Boundless

Zainab Hussain

BookLeaf Publishing

Presentation by *BookLeaf Publishing*

Web: www.bookleafpub.com

E-mail: info@bookleafpub.com

ISBN: 9789357441056

First edition 2023

This book is dedicated to you, my fellow survivors.

May it give you comfort, validation and hope in your darkest moments, and above all, may it remind you of the power of loving yourself.

ACKNOWLEDGEMENT

I offer gratitude for the painful moments in life which made me who I am today.
I offer gratitude for the poetry which enabled me to heal.
I offer gratitude for the love in my life, which keeps me going.

PREFACE

Boundless is a book about power- how it is lost, and how it can be found again. For years, I had been giving my power away, and it wasn't until I reached a breaking point that I realized just how much I had been doing it. I wrote this book because I wanted to take my power back by accepting my experiences instead of hiding them. I used to be too ashamed of my failed relationship to talk about it, but the more I wrote, the more powerful I felt. When I allowed myself to be vulnerable and share my feelings, I started to see things differently- I found myself challenging the self-critical voice in my head and recognizing the successes hidden behind every so-called "failures".

Writing these poems helped me put my experiences into perspective, and center my narrative around myself. By giving more importance to external validation than my own perception of myself, I lost my power as well as the confidence to wield it. I had gotten so used to minimizing myself, putting myself last and suppressing my needs that it became the default setting for all my relationships (romantic and platonic alike). All my life, I had been molding myself into whatever I needed to be in order to be admired and loved, and while that survival mechanism helped me cope, somewhere deep down in my heart, I knew it was hurting me. A part of me knew that I was self-sabotaging but didn't feel strong enough to break out of that pattern…Yet.

Having to teach myself the basics of self-love and retrain my brain was overwhelming, but once I realized how much my past was controlling me, I couldn't just keep digging myself deeper into the hole I was in. I saw that I was on a destructive path and so step by step, I started making changes. I started facing my fears one by one: stage-fright, birds, talking to strangers, etc… and soon enough, they started to feel a little less frightening. One positive thought at a time, I pulled myself out of that hole and even though I am still terrified of falling back into it, I refuse to put my life on hold until I "feel better".

The day I worked up the courage to perform my poetry in front of a room full of strangers was the day I stopped feeling like a helpless victim and started feeling like the survivor I was, and this book is named after that very first poem. As a person with generalized anxiety disorder as well as a stutter, this was one of my greatest fears, and I still don't know how I overcame it, but I hope that reading this book will inspire you to do the same.

These poems are about embracing your intrinsic power and learning to give love to yourself first and foremost. As you read, I encourage you to reflect on the question: "what makes me powerful?"

Should you feel empowered to do so, I welcome you to share your reflections with me by sending them to @storiesuntold_poetry on any of my social media platforms.

I look forward to hearing from you!

Chapter 1: The Nightmare

Frostbite

Oh, brilliant summer sunshine!
Oh, deeply invigorating heat!
Oh, effervescent rays of light!
Are we finally destined to meet?

The frost has reigned for far too long;
the once-splendid meadow lay lifeless.
Even the birds refuse to sing their songs,
here, in this lonely and desolate forest.

Though eager for you I once was,
my optimism was lost with time,
for trapped within calamity's jaws,
I abandoned all hope for sunshine.

To me you were the stuff of fiction,
nothing but stories from an idle mind;
yet here you are, with full conviction,
At my most desperate moment in time.

Alas!
My heart is brittle and may not melt,
for the frost has spread to every crevice,
and enchanted as I may be by your spell,
In all my years, I've known only darkness.

Please Don’t Hurt Me

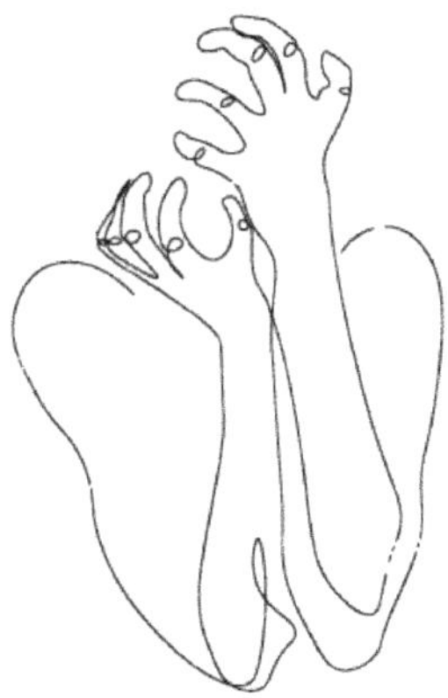

How do I tell you
that I’m afraid to love you?
How do I put into words
the paralyzing fear of being hurt?
How am I supposed to confess
that I’m spiraling into madness?

I wish I could tell you how alone I feel
and ask you to be patient while I heal.
I want to be as brave as you think I am;
deep down, I know you deserve a chance,
but with so many scars covering my back,
it just can’t take any more stabs.

How am I supposed to show you my pain
when I'm terrified it will scare you away?

The harder you try, the more I worry
that someday you'll realize you don't want me,
because my poor little heart is so badly bruised,
and love is easy to give but harder to lose.

Ye of Little Faith

I don't know why you think,
you should hide your true self.
If you can't tell me your secrets,
then who else will you tell?

I don't know why you think,
you need to put me on a pedestal.
You look at me like I'm a Goddess,
but I'm only human after all.

I don't know why you think,
that you aren't good enough.
I don't know why it's so hard,
for you to have faith in us.

I don’t know why you think,
that you shouldn’t be mine.
Haven’t you seen enough to know,
that our love can stand the test of time?

Trauma Bonds

I blame myself for loving too deeply;
I've put myself at a disadvantage.
I know you can't resist me,
and you know I can't resist a challenge.

We both drive each other crazy,
but what we have is so special,
that I accept apology after apology,
and every mistake is forgiven.
All you have to do is look at me,
and I forget anything ever happened.

You have hurt me profoundly,
and keep taking me for granted,
yet I refuse to admit defeat;
I refuse to see you haunted.

Why can't I give up on you?
Is it because I'm broken too?

Nothing Left to Give

I loved the feeling of being needed.
You needed me like you needed tea-
you consumed and indulged,
then complained when you got jittery.

You kept coming back for more,
knowing you couldn't handle the responsibility,
and I kept pouring myself into you,
until finally,
I was left empty.

Unworthy

I can't forget the sound of your voice.
I'm still haunted by the echo of your outburst,
but I also can't forget how you looked
at me, like I was the center of your universe.

I loved all of you, inside and out,
ignoring every red flag and every doubt.
I thought fate had brought us together,
so we could both heal each other,
but you took advantage of my care,
taking my love without giving any in return.

I lost myself in you,
And forgot myself in us,
But it made no difference to you.
Even now that I am gone,
you don’t ask for forgiveness.

Could it be because deep down,
you know you’re not worthy of it?

Siren Song

This has to stop- I must set myself free.
No more of your venomous words,
coated in a deceptive layer of honey.

How can hearing your voice feel so good,
When the words you speak are laced with
poison?

Your siren song has mesmerized,
entranced and shackled my mind,
but it has to stop- this is the last time.

There will always be things I still want to say,
but you have no answers
to the questions keeping me awake.

You have nothing left to offer me,
this experiment has failed repeatedly,
so it’s time for me to accept reality-
It’s time to let go and set myself free.

Frozen in Time

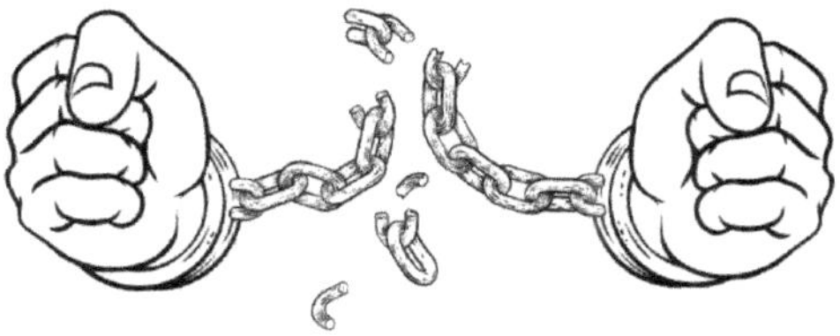

I never seem to learn my lesson;
the song remains the same-
I kneel once more to my emotions;
my heart refuses to be tamed.

If only I was given a chance,
to wipe the slate and start anew,
to end this cursed song and dance,
there is nothing I wouldn't do.

Time and space are my allies now,
in this battle of heart versus mind;
time and space will show me how,
to free myself from these shackles of mine.

Sticks and Stones May Break my Bones, but Words Will Never Hurt Me

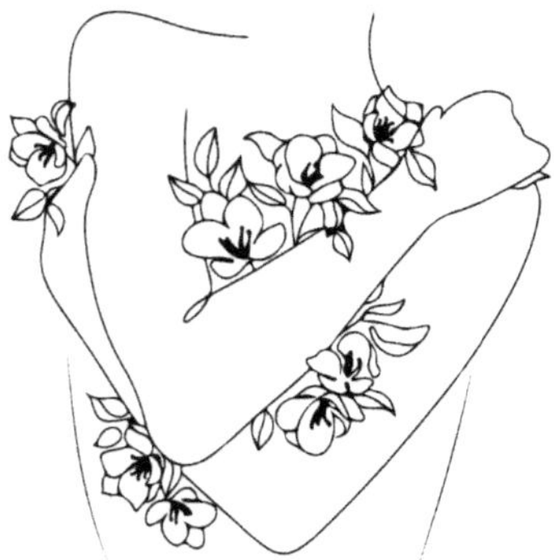

"Sticks and stones" was my mantra,
as I willed myself to grow tougher skin;
maybe if I kept saying it over and over,
it would protect me like an exoskeleton.

Time slowed down in those painful moments;
each vile word cut me like a knife.
I wished for death, so it could be over;
I had no energy left to fight.

But words aren’t sticks or stones or knives,
and one day, I decided that they couldn’t hurt
me-
despite the pain, I had to live my life,
and that was the day I started to heal.

Goodbye

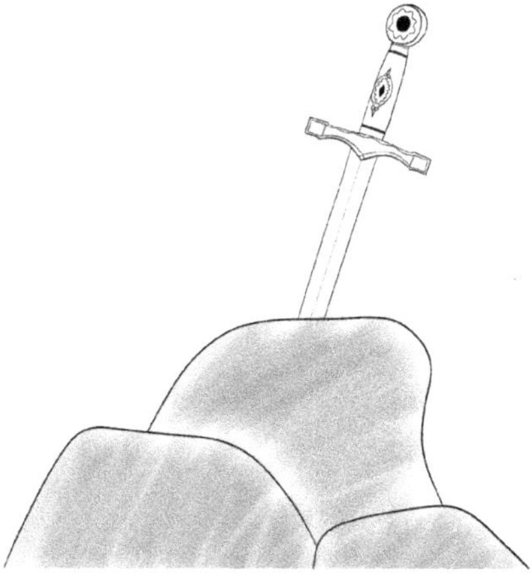

I can't stop the bleeding;
this wound isn't healing.
I'm tired of pulling,
at the knife in my chest-
like the sword in the stone,
It is testing my strength.

I have to do this alone;
I have to pull it out myself.
I have to be my own hero,
No one else can fulfill my quest.

Right now, I may feel helpless,
overwhelmed by the journey ahead,
but if I have made it this far,
then I can survive what's next.
Right now, it may feel hopeless,
but someday, I will forget,
how I gave you my heart,
and watched you shatter it.

I Don't Need My Love Back

I'll call it charity-
every kind word,
every tight hug,
every nursed wound,
every gentle touch,
every act of love,
visible or invisible,
every hour of time,
or ounce of energy,
that I won't get back,
I'll call it charity.

Call it my donation,
to a soul needing salvation,
an act of pity,
for a broken person.

After all, you must be in need of it,
if you insist on suffering,
and refusing
to accept my help.

I kept waiting,
hoping you'd change your ways,
but this was your last chance,
I'm done playing games.

This was my final deposit,
into your love bank.
It's time for me to cut my losses,
and accept that it is too late,
for you to change.

We'll never be even,
so you can keep
what you've been given.
I won't come to collect,
on your many debts,
because my time is too precious,
to be wasted on revenge.

You Did This to Yourself

My tears are an endless supply of ink,
flowing onto pages and pages of poetry.

My broken heart will break your heart,
with words so passionate and powerful,
they will make you regret hurting me.

I will stab you with each phrase,
and turn the knife with each comma.
Every word, so well-chosen, well-placed,
will be the salt I rub into your wound,
before I leave you,
with your self-inflicted pain.

Chapter 2: The Awakening

Lifting the Veil

I did not feel strong,
when I made the call.
I did not feel brave,
for walking away.
I did not feel pride,
for saying goodbye.
I did not feel triumphant,
for shedding my burden.
I will not pretend that it was easy,
to break free.

The loneliness was overwhelming,
aches and pains ravaged my body;

everyone could see that I was crumbling,
weeks passed before I could eat or sleep.
All the things I loved were now triggering,
like eating waffles or going to the beach;
the dark tunnel of despair felt never-ending,
But a distant light kept whispering to me,
pushing me forward.

I longed to go back,
and relive the fantasy,
but once the veil was lifted,
what I saw couldn't be unseen.
There was nothing to go back to,
because it was all just a dream.

So I did the only thing I could do:
I waited...

I waited for father time,
to mend my broken heart.

Day after day, night after night,
I waited for the moment,
when I finally felt strong,
brave,
proud
and triumphant.

This is that moment.

I Confess…

I'm not innocent-
I felt so powerful
every time I convinced
you to be something you were not.

I'm not oblivious-
I was using you to escape
all the noise in my head
and all that was causing me pain.

I'm not perfect-
but I think I deserved better
than to be abandoned
after everything we went through together.

I'm not as wise
as I thought I was,
but now that I've seen the light
I won't crawl back into the dark.

I see
the error of my ways,
I accept
my weaknesses,
I learn
from my mistakes,
and I vow
never to repeat them.

I pray
for healing,
I work
towards growth,
I honor
my feelings,

and I hold on to hope,
because every ending
has to lead to a new beginning.

Addicted

I don't know what love is.
I know toxic relationships,
I know codependence
I know unhealthy attachments,
but I don't know what love is.

I believed that I loved you,
because I felt like I would die without you.
I felt like I needed you to survive,
and needed your love to complete my life;

but I was an addict and you were my drug,
and now I know that that is not love.

I still don't know what exactly love is,
but thanks to you,
at least I know what it is not.

A Word of Advice

Youth is a blessing and a curse,
a mandatory period of confusion,
for only through suffering can we learn,
what it truly means to be human.

Heartbreak is a rite of passage-
every person must endure the agony,
of having their heart crushed,
and finding the strength to continue on their
journey.

Young love is bold and brave,
it's seeing life in color for the first time;
it feels like nothing will ever be the same,
but that's because it makes you blind.

So take my advice,
and learn from your mistakes, child.
Don’t chase after perfection,
because you’re only human.
Don’t doubt your strength,
because you had a moment of weakness,
Don’t let your pain make you forget,
all that you have accomplished.
Don’t be afraid,
to open up your heart,
because even if you get hurt,
you are brave enough,
to survive it.

Fall Down 7 Times, Stand Up 8

Sometimes I wonder why I bother,
when I already know how the story ends-
suffering and I always find each other,
like cursed lovers fighting and making up again.

I hide and I am found,
I run and I am caught,
I fight and I am struck down,
but still I don't stop.

No matter how many times,
my heart betrays me,
I refuse to give up hope.

Whatever it takes to be happy,
I will do it all and more.

Love Yourself First

It is foolishness to attempt,
to fall in love with another,
while you hold contempt,
for the person in your mirror.

That aching void that you felt,
and tried to fill with his "love",
was your lack of love for yourself,
and the belief that you aren't enough.

Your path was lonely before it crossed his,
so you didn't know any better,
but not everyone deserves your gifts,
they must be earned and sought after.

You couldn’t see your own beauty,
and you never understood your worth,
so how could you not fall for his trickery,
when he said all the things you’d never heard?

It will always be difficult to let go,
but there is more for you to seek,
than external sources of validation,
or a “love” that is temporary.

What is Hope?

Hope is like the ocean:
strong and terrifying,
yet peaceful and soothing.

Like some waves are larger than others,
some hopes are greater than others-
it is in the constant pushing and pulling,
that we find ourselves existing.

One Day at a Time

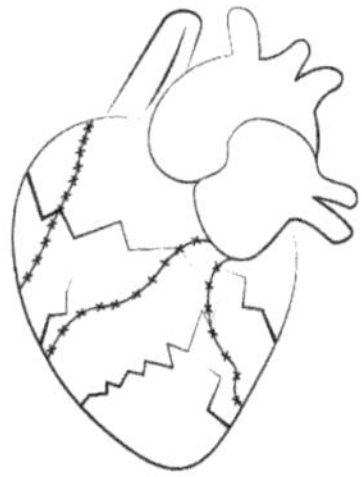

I used to count the days,
now that I'm a bit stronger,
I can count the weeks,
since our last night together.

I believed that I needed you,
now that I'm a bit wiser,
I see that that's not true;
without you, I feel better.

I thought I was living a dream,
now that I'm a bit older,
I see that it was just a fantasy-
there was no "happily ever after".

I ripped my heart out of my chest,
and handed it over to someone else,
but now that I'm stronger, wiser and older,
I know better.

Chasing after Love

Self-love is that bright little firefly,
which I chase through the dark night-
mesmerized by its radiant glow,
everything in me calls me to follow;

I chase and chase to the ends of the Earth,
I pray and pray that I don't get hurt-
this broken bond is my perpetual curse,
as I continue down the road to self-worth.

Boundless

Our love may have died,
murdered at your hands,
but I will survive,
as I always have.
This story is about me,
and my immense capacity for love,
even though it is a tragedy,
and not the romance I thought it was.
In the end, it will be good,
because I know that's what I was-
I was caring and compassionate,
selfless in every aspect,
I was thoughtful and considerate,
understanding and forgiving,
patient and supportive-

I was all the things you needed,
and I saw the joy I brought you,
I witnessed the healing touch,
of my gentle heart,
and that's what this story is all about.
It's about how tender I was,
even though I was hurting,
how loving I was,
even though I was broken,
how hopeful I was,
when everything seemed hopeless-
this is the story of my power,
which I've discovered, is boundless.

My Promise

I swear,
by the blood
In my veins,
by the scar
which remains,
by the truth

born from pain:
my time will come;
I will learn to love again.

Love & Light

I never seem to have
many uplifting words to write.
The stories that my poems tell,
don't paint a picture of delight.
But there is calm in the eye of the storm,
there is method to the madness,
deep down, somewhere there is hope,
for liberation from the sadness.
These words are from the light,
of joy, gratitude and abundance,
which illuminate the dark nights,
and elicit courage and resilience-
whispered by my Higher Power into my heart,
these words are my Noah's ark,

in the unrelenting storm of life:
I affirm that my value is incalculable.
I recognize my beauty, inside and out.
I validate my experience, even when it's painful.
I respect myself, and choose who I will allow,
to drink from my well and nourish themselves.
I affirm that I am triumphant,
as I look back at all the hills I've climbed.
I recognize how incredibly radiant,
I can be when I allow myself to shine.

Take a Breath

Life enjoys trying and testing your strength.
It'll take you on journeys you will not like,
so remember to stop, and take a breath.

With time you will grow, as will the breadth
of your knowledge, but life doesn't give us time.
Life enjoys trying and testing our strength.

You will likely have to go to great lengths,
and endure much pain to do what is right.
Just remember to stop, and take a breath.

If you fail a third, fourth or even a tenth
time, don't ever give up without a fight.
Life enjoys trying and testing your strength.

You might not have vast power or wealth,
but you don't need all that to be alright;
so remember to stop, and take a breath.

Live every moment before your death.
Live, before the darkness engulfs your light.
Life enjoys trying and testing your strength,
so remember to stop, and take a breath.

Trailblazing

The details of the story,
are inconsequential,
the nuances of every,
manipulation and betrayal,
don't deserve to be held in memory-
the space I hold, is only for myself.

I hold space for my existence.
I celebrate my evolution.
I forgive myself for my mistakes.
I no longer chase retribution.
I contemplate my blessings.
I live each day with intention.
I manifest my successes,
and create the future I envision.

I live here, and now,
present in this moment.
My heart is open,
I am ready to be showered,
with good fortune.
Challenges are welcome,
to try to detract me,
but I will shoulder my burdens,
with grace and dignity.
I will walk with my head held high,

with new-found confidence,
because my heart and mind,
are finally in alignment;
I have never felt more alive,
than I do, in this moment.

So don't ask me what I've done,
or where all I have been;
ask me instead, what I am doing,
and where I go from here.
Ask me what I will accomplish,
and what adventures lay ahead,
because the new me is prepared,
to blaze trails you've never imagined.

Love Letter to my Future Self

I love you,
today, tomorrow and forever.
I love you,
for your heart,
and spirit,
for your courage,
and brilliance,
for your empathy,
and resilience,
for your generosity,
and kindness;
for the way you spread joy,
and positivity.

I love you,
because you deserve to be loved,
today, tomorrow and forever.

www.ingramcontent.com/pod-product-compliance
Lightning Source LLC
Chambersburg PA
CBHW051737130826
49812CB00033B/896
9789357441056